Thich Nhat Hanh is a world-renowned writer, poet, scholar and Zen Buddhist monk, who lives mostly in the monastic community he founded in France. The author of the *New York Times* bestseller *Anger* and the classic work *The Miracle of Mindfulness*, as well as numerous other books, he conducts public workshops and peace-making retreats throughout the world. He was nominated for the Nobel Peace Prize in 1967.

www.plumvillage.org

By the same author

Silence

Anger

Being Peace

Breathe! You Are Alive

Creating True Peace

Fear

Fragrant Palm Leaves

Going Home

The Heart of the Buddha's Teaching

Living Buddha, Living Christ

The Miracle of Mindfulness

THICH NHAT HANH

HOW TO WALK

'THE FATHER OF MINDFULNESS'
IRISH TIMES

LONDON • SYDNEY • AUCKLAND • JOHANNESBURG

7 9 10 8 6

Rider, an imprint of Ebury Publishing,
20 Vauxhall Bridge Road,
London SW1V 2SA

Rider is part of the Penguin Random House group
of companies whose addresses can be found at
global.penguinrandomhouse.com

Penguin
Random House
UK

First published in Britain by Rider in 2016
Published in the United States by Parallax Press in 2015

www.penguin.co.uk

Illustrations by Jason DeAntonis

A CIP catalogue record for this book is available from the
British Library

ISBN 9781846045165

Printed and bound in Great Britain by Clays Ltd,
St Ives PLC

CONTENTS

The first thing to do is to lift your foot.
Breathe in. Put your foot down in front of
you, first your heel and then your toes.
Breathe out. Feel your feet solid on the
Earth. You have already arrived.

We frequently walk with the sole purpose of getting from one place to another. But where are we in between? With every step, we can feel the miracle of walking on solid ground. We can arrive in the present moment with every step.

When we first learned to walk, we walked just to enjoy walking. We walked and discovered each moment as we encountered it. We can learn to walk that way again.

NOTES ON WALKING

YOU HAVE ARRIVED

When you walk, arrive with every step.
That is walking meditation. There's nothing
else to it.

WHY WALK?

People ask me, "Why do you do walking meditation?" The best answer I can give is, "Because I like it." Every step makes me happy. There's no use in doing walking meditation if you're not going to enjoy every step you make; it would be a waste of time. The same thing is true with sitting meditation. If someone asked, "What's the use of sitting for hours and hours?" The best answer is, "Because I like sitting." Sitting and walking can bring peace and joy. We have to learn how to sit and walk so that we can produce peace and joy during the time of sitting or the time of walking. We have to learn to walk so that we can enjoy every step. Mindfulness and concentration can bring a higher quality to our breath, to our sitting, and to our steps.

ARRIVING

One of the most profound teachings is also the shortest: "I have arrived." When we return to our breathing, we return to the present moment, our true home. There's no need for us to struggle to arrive somewhere else. We know our final destination is the cemetery. Why are we in a hurry to get there? Why not step in the direction of life, which is in the present moment? If we practice walking meditation for even a few days, we will undergo a deep transformation and learn how to enjoy peace in each moment. We smile, and countless beings throughout the cosmos smile back at us—our peace is so deep. Everything we think, feel, and do has an effect on our ancestors and future generations and reverberates throughout the cosmos.

PRACTICING JOY

We may think of joy as something that happens spontaneously. Few people realize that it needs to be cultivated and practiced in order to grow. Mindfulness is the continuous practice of deeply touching every moment of daily life. To be mindful is to be truly present with your body and your mind, to bring harmony to your intentions and actions, and to be in harmony with those around you. We don't need to make a separate time for this outside of our daily activities. We can practice mindfulness in every moment of the day as we walk from one place to another. When we walk through a door, we know that we're going through a door. Our minds are with our actions.

WALKING ON PLANET EARTH

Walking on this planet is a very wonderful thing to do. When astronauts return to Earth, one of the things that they're most happy to do is to take a walk. Coming back to their home, they can enjoy the grasses, the plants, the flowers, the animals, and the birds with each step. How long do you think they enjoy walking on the Earth after they've returned from space? I'd guess that the first ten days are wonderful. But eventually they get used to it, and maybe a year later they don't feel as happy as they did in the first few months after coming home. Every time we take a step on this Earth, we can appreciate the solid ground underneath us.

I WALK FOR YOU

Many of my ancestors and many of my friends from my generation have already passed away. A good friend of mine is in a wheelchair and can't walk. Another friend has such pain in his knees that he can't walk up and down stairs. So I walk for them. When I breathe in, I say to myself, "It's wonderful that I am still able to walk like this." With that awareness, I can enjoy every step. I say, "I am alive!" Mindfulness reminds me to notice and enjoy that my body is alive and strong enough for me to walk.

SLEEPWALKING

We're in such a rush, looking for happiness
in one place and then another. We walk like
sleepwalkers, without any enjoyment of
what we are actually doing. We are walking,
but in our minds we are already doing
something else: planning, organizing, worrying.
There is no more need to run. Every time
we return our attention to our breath and
our steps, it's as if we wake up. Every step
brings us back to the here and the now.
We can touch the Earth and see the sky
and notice all the wonders in between. In
each step there is the possibility of mindfulness, concentration, and insight.

ENLIGHTENMENT

To enjoy walking meditation isn't difficult
at all. You don't need ten years of practicing mindful walking to be enlightened. You
need only a few seconds. You just need
to become aware that you're walking.
Awareness is already enlightenment. Each
of us is capable of being mindful of our
in-breath and our out-breath. When you
breathe in, be aware that you're breathing in. Be aware that you have a body, that
you're breathing in and nourishing that
body. Be aware that your feet are strong
enough for you to enjoy walking. That is
also enlightenment. When you breathe out,
be aware of the air leaving your body. Be
aware that you are alive. This awareness
can bring you so much happiness.

WALKING IN THE AIRPORT

When I go to the airport, I like to arrive
early so that I can do walking meditation
before the flight. About thirty years ago
I was walking in the Honolulu airport.
Someone came up to me and asked, "Who
are you; what is your spiritual tradition?"
I said, "Why do you ask?" And he said,
"Because I see that the way you walk is so
different than the way others walk. It's so
peaceful and relaxed." He had approached
me simply because of the way I walked.
I hadn't given a speech or a conference.
With every step you make, you can create
peace within yourself and give joy to
other people.

CLIMBING THE MOUNTAIN

I once traveled with a delegation to China and climbed Wutai Shan, a famous mountain there. The path to the top is very steep, and usually people arrive exhausted. There are 1,080 steps to climb. Before setting out, I suggested our delegation breathe, make a step, relax; breathe, make another step, and relax. Our intention was to climb the mountain in a way that we could enjoy each moment of the climbing. Every ten steps or so we would sit down, look around, breathe, and smile. We didn't need to arrive; we arrived in every step, with peace, stillness, solidity, and freedom. When we got to the top, everybody was so happy and full of energy. Every step, even uphill, can bring mindfulness, concentration, joy, and insight.

WALKING WITH
DANIEL BERRIGAN

One day in New York City, I invited Daniel
Berrigan, the Catholic father, poet, and peace
activist, to go for a walk in Central Park. I
told him, "No talking, just walking." Father
Berrigan is much taller than I am and his legs
are very long; one of his steps was equal to
two of mine. We started out together but
after a few steps he was way ahead. When he
turned around and saw I wasn't next to him,
he stopped and waited. I didn't rush. I was
determined to walk slowly and mindfully at
my own pace. I was determined to pay close
attention to my steps and breath, otherwise
I knew I would lose myself and get carried
away in the idea that there was a rush. Each
time I caught up, we would walk together for
a little while and then he would get in front

again. Each time, I would keep my own pace. Later, he came to visit me in France and he had a chance to learn and practice walking meditation. He was able to walk without rushing, even when he returned to New York.

WALKING IN BEAUTY

You can walk mindfully on the busiest
street. Sometimes, though, it's helpful to
practice in a park or some other beautiful, quiet place. Walk slowly, but not so
slowly that you draw too much attention
to yourself. This is a kind of invisible practice. Enjoy nature and your own serenity
without making others uncomfortable or
making a show of it. If you see something
that you want to stop and appreciate—the
blue sky, the hills, a tree, or a bird—just
stop, and continue to breathe in and out
mindfully. If we don't continue to breathe
consciously, sooner or later our thinking
will settle back in, and the bird and the tree
will disappear.

RUNNING

In every one of us there's a tendency to run. There's a belief that happiness is not possible here and now, so we have the tendency to run into the future in order to look for happiness. That habit energy may have been transmitted to us by our father, our mother, or our ancestors. Running has become a habit. Even in our dreams we continue to run and look for something. The practice of mindfulness helps us to stop running and see that everything we have been looking for is here. Many of us have been running all our lives. One mindful step can help us to stop running. When the mind is focused on breathing and walking, we are unifying body, speech, and mind, and we are already home.

PLACE TO PLACE

It is possible to enjoy every step we make, not only during walking meditation, but at any time, whenever you need to move from one place to another place, no matter how short the distance is. If you're walking five steps, then walk those five steps mindfully, feeling your stability with every step. When you climb the stairs, climb each step with joy. With each step, you can generate your best energy and transfer it out into the world.

SILENCE

In Plum Village, the practice center where I live in southwest France, we don't talk when we walk. This helps us fully enjoy walking one hundred percent. If you talk a lot, then it's difficult for you to experience your steps deeply, and you won't enjoy them very much. The same is true when you drink a cup of tea: if you're concentrated and you focus your attention on the cup of tea, then the cup of tea becomes a great joy. Mindfulness and concentration bring about pleasure and insight.

WALKING FOR OUR ANCESTORS AND FUTURE GENERATIONS

All our ancestors and all future generations are present in us all the time. Happiness is not an individual matter. As long as the ancestors in us are still suffering, we can't be happy and we will transmit that suffering to our children and their children. When we walk, we can walk for our ancestors and future generations. Maybe they had to walk with sorrow; perhaps they were forced to march or migrate. When we walk freely, we are walking for them. If we can take one step freely and happily, touching the Earth mindfully, then we can take one hundred steps like that. We do it for ourselves and for all previous and future generations. We all arrive at the same time and find peace and happiness together.

LIFE'S ADDRESS

When you walk mindfully, just enjoy walking. The technique to practice is to walk and just to be exactly where you are, even if you are moving. Your true destination is the here and the now, because only in this moment and in this place is life possible. The address of all the great beings is "here and now." The address of peace and light is also "here and now." You know where to go. Every in-breath, every out-breath, every step you make should bring you back to that address.

INVEST YOUR WHOLE BODY

Invest one hundred percent of yourself into making a step. Touching the ground with your foot, you produce the miracle of being alive. You make yourself real and the Earth real with each step. The practice should be very strong and determined. You are protecting yourself from the habit energy that is always pushing you to run and to get lost in thinking. Bring all your attention down to the soles of your feet, and touch the Earth as though you are kissing the Earth with your feet. Each step is like the seal of an emperor on a decree. Walk as though you imprint your solidity, your freedom, and your peace on the Earth.

STOPPING AND FINDING CALM

Walking is a wonderful way to calm down
when we are upset. When we walk, if we
focus all our awareness on walking, we are
stopping the thinking, storytelling, blaming,
and judging that goes on in our heads and
takes us away from the present moment.
To stop the incessant thinking in the mind,
it helps to focus on the body. When things
aren't going well, it's good to stop the
thinking in order to prevent the unpleasant,
destructive energies from continuing.
Stopping does not mean repressing; it
means, first of all, calming. If we want the
ocean to be calm, we don't throw away its
water. Without the water, nothing is left.
When we notice the presence of anger,
fear, and agitation in us, we don't need to

throw them away. We only have to breathe in and out consciously and take a mindful step. Allow yourself to sink deeply into the here and the now, because life is available only in the present moment. This alone is enough to calm the storm.

RECOVERING OUR SOVEREIGNTY

When we are pushed and pulled in many different directions, we lose our sovereignty. We're not free. Don't allow yourself to be carried away anymore. Resist. Each mindful step is a step toward freedom. This kind of freedom is not political freedom. It's freedom from the past, from the future, from our worries and our fears.

ONLY WALK

When you walk, only walk. Don't think. Don't talk. If you want to talk to others or have a snack, you can stop in order to do so. In that way, you'll be fully present for the walking and also fully present for the person you're speaking to when you talk. You can sit down somewhere to make your phone call in peace, to eat your food, or drink your juice in mindfulness.

WALKING IS A MIRACLE

Our true home is in the present moment. To live in the present moment is a miracle. When I breathe in and become fully alive, I see myself as a miracle. When I look at an orange mindfully, I see the orange is a miracle. When I peel an orange mindfully, I see that eating an orange is also a miracle. The fact that you are still alive is a miracle. So miracles are the things that you perform several times each day with the power of mindfulness. The miracle is not to walk on water. The miracle is to walk on the green Earth in the present moment, to appreciate the peace and beauty that are available now. I perform this miracle every time I walk. You too can perform the miracle of walking any time you want.

MOTHER EARTH

When we walk, we touch the Earth. It's a great happiness to be able to touch the Earth, the mother of all beings on this planet. While practicing walking, we should be aware that we are walking on a living being that is supporting not just us, but all of life. A lot of harm has been done to the Earth, so now it is time to kiss the ground with our feet, with our love. While you are walking, smile—be in the here and the now. By doing so, you transform the place where you are walking into a paradise.

IMPRINTING ON THE EARTH

We walk all the time, but usually we only walk because we have to, so that we can get to the next thing. When we walk like that, we print anxiety and sorrow on the Earth. We have the capability to walk in a way that we only imprint peace and serenity on the Earth. Every one of us can do that. Any child can do that. If we can take one step like that, we can take two, three, four, and five. When we are able to take one step peacefully, happily, we are creating one more step of peace and happiness for the whole of humankind.

TOUCHING PEACE

The possibility of peace is all around us, in the world and in nature. Peace is also within us, in our bodies and our spirits. The act of walking will water the seeds of peace that are already there inside us. Our mindful steps help us cultivate the habit of touching peace in each moment.

A CONTRACT WITH
THE STAIRCASE

Make an agreement with the flight of stairs
you use most often. Decide to always
practice walking meditation on those
stairs, going up and going down; don't
climb those stairs absentmindedly. If you
commit to this and then realize you have
climbed several steps in forgetfulness, go
back down and climb up them again. Over
twenty years ago, I signed such an agreement with my stairs, and it has brought me
great joy.

WALKING ON CAPITOL HILL

Once we offered a retreat for Congress members and staff in Washington, D.C., and some of the participants have continued to practice walking meditation every day. Everyone there walks very quickly, so they have had to be diligent to continue practicing what they learned at the retreat, but a couple of them have kept it up. They told me that they always do walking meditation from their office to the place where they cast their vote. They say they can survive better in their environment because of that kind of practice, even during the most difficult and contentious sessions.

WALKING WITH OTHERS

I have been in crowds of two or three thousand people practicing walking meditation
together. It is very powerful. Everybody
makes just one step at a time and is wholly
concentrated on that step. Please arrange
things so that during your day you have
many chances to try walking mindfully on
your own. You can also practice walking
with others to get support. You can ask a
friend to go with you. If you're with a child,
you can take the hand of the child and
walk with him or her.

A KUNG FU NOTEBOOK

The words "kung fu" mean daily diligent practice. You don't have to be doing martial arts to have a daily practice. Walking can be that practice. At the end of the day, you might like to review and write about the practice you've had during the day, what you noticed about walking, breathing, smiling, or speaking. It would be a pity if you spent the whole day without enjoying walking. You have feet, and if you don't make use of them it's a loss and a waste. Someone is telling you now so that in the future you cannot say: "No one told me that it was important to enjoy using my feet."

THE FRUIT OF OUR PRACTICE

When you walk with a lot of tenderness
and happiness on this beautiful planet, you
are living peace. In Buddhist practice, it is
said that the *bodhisattva* Avalokiteshvara,
a being with great compassion, spends all
of his or her time on Earth enjoying walking, riding the waves of birth and death,
and smiling. We should be able to do the
same. If we can truly arrive and feel at
home while walking, that is the practice—
but it is also the fruit of our practice. These
are moments that are worth living.

PUTTING ON YOUR SHOES

Every day you put on your shoes and walk somewhere. So every day you have an opportunity to practice mindfulness that doesn't take any extra time. You take off your shoes and you put them on. This is also a time for practice and enjoyment.

THE BUDDHA'S FEET

If you empower your feet with the energy of mindfulness, your feet become the Buddha's feet. You may have seen people who walk with the Buddha's feet; you can tell just by watching them. It's very easy. If you have an electric car, it takes a few hours to recharge it. But to empower your feet with the energy of mindfulness, you don't even need half an hour. The power of mindfulness comes right away. It's up to you whether you choose to walk with the feet of the Buddha.

WALKING AND TALKING

Often when we walk, we are already talking to someone next to us, or thinking of what we have to do next, or even staring at our phone, not looking at where we are or where we're going. When you walk, try to just walk. Try not to walk and talk at the same time. If you need to say something, stop altogether and say it. It won't take too much more time. Then, after you finish talking, you can resume walking.

WALKING IN PRISON

I have a friend, a nun, who graduated from
Indiana University in English literature,
and then practiced as a nun in Vietnam.
She was arrested by the police and put
in prison because of her public calls for
peace. She tried her best to practice walking and sitting meditation in her prison
cell. It was difficult, because during the
daytime, if the guards saw her practicing
meditation, they thought of it as a pro-
vocative action. She had to wait until they
turned off the light in order to practice.
She did walking meditation, even though
her cell was only ten square feet. In prison,
they stole many freedoms from her, but
they couldn't steal her determination and
her practice.

FINDING EASE

If walking feels difficult or challenging,
stop. Let your breath lead you. Don't force
it. Once, I was in a crowded airport. People
were gathered around me so close that
I couldn't even walk. I couldn't take one
step. I started to push through them, but
then I stopped. I remembered that I didn't
have to do anything. I became so relaxed,
because I felt that the Buddha was walking, not me. If it was me, maybe I wouldn't
have been so relaxed and compassionate
like that. As soon as I stopped and relaxed,
I was able to walk freely. The airport was
still crowded, but I took each step slowly,
with ease and joy.

WALKING FOR OTHERS

Sometimes I say that I walk for my mother or that my father is enjoying walking with me. I walk for my father. I walk for my mother. I walk for my teacher. I walk for my students. Maybe your father never knew how to walk mindfully, enjoying every moment like that. So I do it for him and we both get the benefit.

A LONG WALK

After his enlightenment in Bodhgaya,
the Buddha practiced walking meditation
around the nearby lotus pond. Then,
he wanted to share his insights with his
close friends who were in the Deer Park,
in Sarnath. So he walked from Bodhgaya
to Sarnath to find them. He walked alone
among rice fields and forests. It must
have taken him at least two weeks to get
there, but he enjoyed every step he made.
When the Buddha found his old friends, he
shared his first teaching.

NIRVANA

Nirvana is something that can't be described. You have to taste it for yourself. If you've never eaten kiwi fruit, no one can describe to you how it tastes. The best way to find out is to put a piece of kiwi in your mouth. Then you'll know the taste of kiwi right away. Nirvana is the same. You have to taste nirvana for yourself. Nirvana is available to you right now in every step. You don't need to die in order to enter into it. It's not vague or far away. If every step you make takes you to the shore of free-dom, then you can already taste nirvana.

WALKING HOME

Walking brings the mind and body together. Only when mind and body are united are we truly in the here and the now. When we walk, we come home to ourselves. If you're busy talking while you walk, or planning ahead, you won't enjoy your in-breath and out-breath. You won't enjoy being fully in the present moment. We don't have to force ourselves to breathe in, because we're breathing in and out all the time anyway. We only need to focus our attention on the breath and the walking. In no time at all, you go home to your body, and there you are, well established in the here and the now.

COLLECTIVE ENERGY

When we walk with others, the collective
energy of mindfulness we generate is very
powerful. It helps heal everyone. When
we walk together, producing the energy
of mindfulness, going home to the here
and the now, we can feel paradise right
under our feet; you can see this paradise
all around you.

GENERATING MINDFUL ENERGY

When we walk, we produce the energy of mindfulness. Instead of thinking of this or that, just be aware of the contact between your foot and the ground. If you pay attention to that contact, it's very healing. Don't wait until you have a group or a scheduled time. Every time you need to move from one place to another, you can apply the techniques of walking meditation. From your living room to your kitchen, from your car to your work, take your time and enjoy every step. Stop the thinking, stop the talking, and touch the Earth with your feet. If you enjoy every step, your practice is good.

SOLIDITY

When the past and the future can't pull you away anymore, every step is solid. You are firmly established in the here and the now. Solidity and freedom are the foundation of happiness. If you're not solid, if you're not free, happiness isn't possible. So every step is to cultivate more solidity and freedom. As you walk, you can say to yourself, "I am solid. I am free." This is not autosuggestion or wishful thinking. This is a realization, because if you are well established in the here and the now, you realize this truth with every step.

LETTING GO OF THE PAST

Most of us walk without chains, yet we aren't free. We're tethered to regret and sorrow from the past. We return to the past and continue to suffer. The past is a prison. But now you have the key to unlock the door and arrive in the present moment. You breathe in, you bring your mind home to your body, you make a step, and you arrive in the here and the now. There is the sunshine, the beautiful trees, and the songs of the birds.

TAKING CARE OF THE FUTURE

There are those of us who are prisoners of the future. We don't know what will happen but we worry so much that the future becomes a kind of prison. The real future is made only of one substance, and that is the present. What else can the future be made of? If we know how to take care of the present moment the best we can, that's all we can do to assure ourselves of a good future. We build the future by taking care of the present moment. Taking care of the present moment includes mindful breathing, enjoying your in-breath and out-breath. With each step, you arrive in the future you are making. Make it a future of peace and compassion.

LISTEN TO YOUR LUNGS

Let your own lungs determine your breathing.
Never force your breath. When walking,
match your steps to your breath, not the
other way around. You might begin by taking
two steps for your in-breath and three
steps for your out-breath. If, as you
continue to walk, your lungs say they'd be
happier making three steps while breathing
in and five steps while breathing out, then
you make three steps and five steps. Of
course when you're climbing a hill, the
number of steps you can take with each
breath will naturally be reduced. In walking meditation, I notice I usually breathe
in for four steps and breathe out for six.

But when I climb, I do two steps for each in-breath and three for each out-breath. When it's very steep, I sometimes do one step for every breath in and three, two, or even one for every breath out. We have to adapt. Listening to your body as you walk will help make every step pleasant.

GETTING IN TOUCH

Sometimes when I visit with friends or students from far away, they want to stay in touch. For the last forty years, I haven't used a telephone. Many of us talk a lot on the telephone, but that doesn't mean that we have good communication with the other person. I don't have an email address. But you don't need a phone or a computer to be in touch with me. If you just walk from your home to the bus stop in mindfulness and enjoy every step, we're connected. If you practice mindful breathing and mindful walking, we're connected all the time. When people ask me for my address, I tell them, "It's the here and now."

FORGETFULNESS

We have been living in forgetfulness for many years. Forgetfulness is the opposite of mindfulness. Mindfulness is to remember that life is a wonder; we are here, and we should live our lives deeply. We know that we want to be more present, but very often we don't do it. We need a friend or a teacher to remind us. The Earth can be that teacher. It is always there, greeting your feet, keeping you solid and grounded.

TRAINING OURSELVES

There are those of us who, right in the first session of mindful walking, can already arrive. Others of us find it difficult, because the habit of running is so strong. I remember one day a journalist from Paris came to interview me. He was invited to join us in walking meditation before we had the interview. He suffered very much during the walk. He reported later that it was exhausting. He was so used to running that for him walking mindfully and slowly felt like hard work! So we have to train ourselves in walking. We walk in such a way that every step can help us to stop running the useless race and get in touch with the wonders of life that are available in the here and the now.

EACH STEP IS AN
ACT OF RESISTANCE

Every step is a revolution against busyness. Each mindful step says: "I don't want to run anymore. I want to stop. I want to live my life. I don't want to miss the wonders of life." When you can truly arrive, there is peace in you because you aren't struggling anymore. Each footprint has peace in it, it has the mark "here and now" in it. You may enjoy arriving and feeling at home for three, four, five, or ten minutes, as long as you like. One hour of practice already begins the revolution.

ACKNOWLEDGING THE BODY

We have a physical body, which is a wonder. But this physical body will one day disintegrate. That is the truth we have to accept. On the surface, there is birth and death, being and nonbeing. But if you go more deeply, you recognize that you also have a cosmic body that exists outside of birth and death, being and nonbeing. A wave on the ocean doesn't last very long. A wave's physical body lasts five, ten, or twenty seconds. But the wave has her ocean body, because she comes from the ocean and she will go back to the ocean. If you walk mindfully, if your concentration and insight are powerful, with every step you can touch your cosmic body and you will lose all your fear and uncertainty.

CREATING A HABIT
OF MINDFUL WALKING

Every time you need to go somewhere,
even if it's a very short distance of three
or five steps, you can apply mindful walking. Soon, it will become a habit. You will
find that you are walking mindfully to pick
up the phone or to make your tea. You
may not realize at first why you don't feel
rushed or why you are happier when you
walk in the door. Cultivating a daily habit
of walking meditation is free and it doesn't
take any more time than the walking you
are already doing.

SETTING AN EXAMPLE

When you walk with mindfulness, you set
an example for everyone who sees you,
even if you don't realize it. When we see
you walking with freedom, with peace, with
joy, we may be motivated by the desire to
mirror you. Together, without effort, we
create more of an atmosphere of peace
and happiness.

INTENTION

The intention to enjoy your steps and your breath is not enough; you need mindfulness and insight. If every step you take brings you joy, it's because while making a step you have mindfulness and insight. Without insight, it's impossible for you to enjoy your in-breath and out-breath. You can't force yourself to enjoy your breath or your steps. Breathing mindfully, making steps in awareness, joy comes naturally and easily.

THE SOLE OF YOUR FOOT

You might like to focus your attention on the sole of your foot. Feel the contact between your foot and the ground. You are down there in your foot, not up here in your head. There's a feeling that you are touching the beautiful Mother Earth.

WALKING EVERYWHERE

In the Buddha's time, there were no cars, no trains, no airplanes. From time to time the Buddha used a boat to travel upon or across a river. But mostly he walked. During his forty-five years of teaching, he visited and taught in perhaps fourteen or fifteen countries of ancient India and Nepal. That was a lot of walking. Many of his teachings, many of his insights, came from his time of walking everywhere.

WALKING ALONG THE GANGES

The first time I flew into India, I had fifteen minutes to contemplate the landscape below before landing in the city of Patna. I saw the Ganges River for the first time. As a novice monk, I had learned of the Ganges with its sands, which are too numerous to be counted. Sitting in the airplane, I looked down and I saw the footprints of the Buddha a little bit everywhere all along the banks of the Ganges River. It is certain that the Buddha walked back and forth many times along that river. He walked like that for forty-five years, bringing his wisdom and compassion and sharing his practice of liberation with many people, from kings and ministers to scavengers and the poor.

THE NON-PRACTICE PRACTICE

When the Buddha walked, he didn't seem
to be practicing meditation. He didn't
have access to any special tools; he just
had two feet like the rest of of us, and he
enjoyed walking. The best way to practice
has the appearance of non-practice, but
it's very deep. You don't make any effort;
you don't struggle; you just enjoy walking.
"My practice," the Buddha said in the Sutra
of Forty-Two Chapters, "is the practice
of non-practice, the attainment of non-
attainment." If your practice is natural, if
your practice brings you happiness, that's
the best kind of practice. You don't look
like you're practicing, but you're practicing
very deeply.

INTENTION

Walking meditation is a way to practice moving without a goal or intention. Mindful walking simply means walking while being aware of each step and of our breathing. We can even practice mindful breathing and walking meditation in between business appointments or in the parking lot of the supermarket. We can keep our steps slow, relaxed, and calm. There's no rush, no place to get to, no hurry. Mindful walking can release our sorrows and our worries and help bring peace into body and mind.

LOVING THE EARTH

When we're in love with someone or
something, there's no separation between
ourselves and the person or thing we love.
We do whatever we can for them, and this
brings us great joy and nourishment. When
we see the Earth this way, we will walk
more gently on her.

WALKING OUTSIDE

When we open the door and go out into the fresh air, we can be immediately in touch with the air and the Earth and all the elements around us. When we walk, we know we're not stepping on something inanimate. The ground we're walking on is not inert matter. Understanding the Earth in this way, we can walk on the planet with as much respect and reverence as we would walk when in a house of worship or in any sacred space. We can bring our full awareness to each step. Steps like these have the power to save our lives.

MORNING WALK

Every morning when I wake up and get
dressed, I leave my hut and take a walk.
Usually the sky is still dark and I walk
gently, aware of nature all around me
and the fading stars. When I think of the
Earth and my ability to walk on it, I think,
"I'm going to go out into nature, enjoying
everything beautiful, enjoying all its wonders." My heart is filled with joy.

WALKING IN THE CITY

Try to practice mindful walking in your
daily life. When you go to the bus stop,
make it into a walking meditation. Even
if your surroundings are full of noise and
agitation, you can still walk in rhythm with
your breathing. In the commotion of a big
city, you can still walk with peace, happiness,
and an inner smile. This is what it means to
live fully in every moment of every day of
your life.

THE AWARENESS OF LOVE

Walking mindfully, with love and understanding, we can become deeply aware
of every single thing on this planet. We
notice that the leaves on the trees are a
startling light green in spring, a vibrant
green in summer, rich yellow, orange, and
red in autumn, and then in winter, when the
branches are bare, the trees continue to
stand tall, strong, and beautiful, harboring
life deep inside. Mother Earth receives the
fallen leaves and breaks them down to
create new nourishment for the tree so
that it can continue to grow.

WE DON'T WALK ALONE

When we walk, we're not walking alone. Our parents and ancestors are always walking with us. They're present in every cell of our bodies. So each step that brings us healing and happiness also brings healing and happiness to our parents and ancestors. Every mindful step has the power to transform us and all our ancestors within us, including our animal, plant, and mineral ancestors. We don't walk for ourselves alone. When we walk, we walk for our family and for the whole world.

RETURNING

We don't have to wait until we die to return
to Mother Earth. In fact, we're in the process
of going back to Mother Earth right now.
Thousands of cells in our bodies are dying
each moment, and new ones are being
born. Whenever we breathe, whenever we
walk, we are returning to the Earth.

GRATITUDE

When we do walking meditation, we
can take each step in gratitude and joy
because we know that we're walking on
the Earth. We can walk with gentle steps,
in reverence to Mother Earth who gave us
birth and of whom we are a part. The Earth
we're walking on is sacred. We should be
very respectful because we know we're
walking on our mother. Wherever we
walk, we're walking on Mother Earth, so
wherever we are can be a holy sanctuary.

WHOLE BODY, WHOLE MIND

Don't pretend you're walking mindfully
when in reality you're planning your grocery
shopping or your next meeting. Walk with
your whole body and mind. Each step
contains insight. Each step has happiness.
Each step has love—love and compassion
for the Earth and for all beings, as well as
for ourselves. Why do we walk like that?
To be in touch with the great Earth, to be
in touch with the world around us. When
we're in touch, when we're fully aware
of the wonder of walking on the Earth,
each step nourishes and heals us. Thirty
steps taken with this kind of insight are
thirty opportunities to nourish and heal
ourselves.

WAKING UP

Walking meditation is a way of waking up to the wonderful moment we are living in. If our minds are caught up and preoccupied with our worries and our suffering, or if we distract ourselves with other things while walking, we can't practice mindfulness; we can't enjoy the present moment. We're missing out on life. But if we're awake, then we'll see this is a wonderful moment that life has given us, the only moment in which life is available. We can value each step we take, and each step can bring us happiness because we're in touch with life, with the source of happiness, and with our beloved planet.

WALKING INSTEAD OF DRIVING

Sometimes we don't really need to use the car, but because we want to get away from ourselves, we go down and start the car. If we recite the phrase, "Before starting the car, I know where I am going," it can be like a flashlight—we may see that we don't need to go anywhere. You cannot escape yourself, wherever you go. Sometimes it's better to turn the engine off and go out for a walk. It may be more pleasant to do.

MASSAGING THE EARTH

When we walk mindfully, our feet are mas-
saging the Earth. We sow seeds of joy and
happiness with each step. With each step,
a flower blooms.

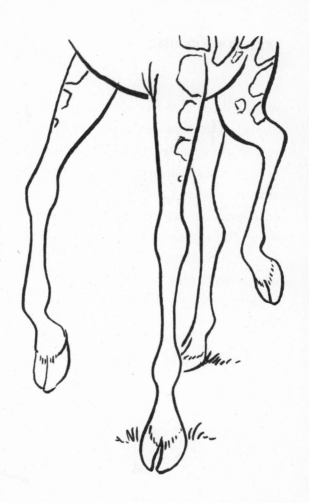

TAKING YOUR TIME

Allow enough time to walk. If you usually
give yourself three minutes to get from
your car to your door, give yourself eight
or ten minutes. I always give myself an
extra hour when I go to the airport so that
I can practice walking meditation when I'm
there. Sometimes my friends want to keep
visiting right up to the last minute, but I
always resist. I tell them that I need the
time, and I say my good-byes early.

WALKING IS A CELEBRATION

When you walk, if you are aware that you are alive, that is already enlightenment. You are aware that you have a body; that is already enlightenment. You are aware that your feet are strong enough for you to enjoy walking; that is also enlightenment. When you walk, it can be a celebration. When you breathe like that, you are celebrating life.

WALKING WITH CHILDREN

Walking with children is a wonderful way to practice mindfulness. From time to time, a child may want to run ahead and then wait for you to catch up. A child is a bell of mindfulness, reminding us how marvelous life is. We can remind children that walking meditation is a wonderful way for them to calm down when they have strong feelings or are upset. We can walk with them without saying anything, just walking alongside. Our own breath is a gentle reminder for them to breathe with each step.

WALKING
MEDITATIONS

BREATHING AND WALKING

Our in-breath tends to be a little bit shorter than our out-breath. When you breathe in, take two or three steps. This is determined by your lungs. If your lungs want two steps as you breathe in, then give exactly two steps. If you feel better with three steps, then give yourself three steps. When you breathe out, you also listen to your lungs and let them determine how many steps you make while breathing out. In the beginning, practice two steps for the in-breath and three for the out-breath: *two, three; two, three; two, three*. Later on it may be *three, four* or *three, five*. If you feel you need to make one more step while breathing in, then allow yourself to enjoy one more step. When you feel that you want to make one more step while breathing out, then allow yourself to add another step as you breathe out. Every step should be enjoyable.

LETTING THE BUDDHA WALK

Several years ago, I was in Seoul, South Korea, to lead a large walking meditation in the city. When the time came to lead the walk, I found it very difficult to walk because hundreds of cameramen were closing in. There was no path to walk at all. I said, "Dear Buddha, I give up. You walk for me." The Buddha came right away and he walked. The path became clear. After this experience, I wrote a series of poems that can be used any time, but especially when walking or breathing is challenging.

Let the Buddha breathe,
Let the Buddha walk.
I don't have to breathe,
I don't have to walk.

The Buddha is breathing,
The Buddha is walking.
I enjoy the breathing,
I enjoy the walking.

Buddha is the breathing,
Buddha is the walking.
I am the breathing,
I am the walking.

There is only the breathing,
There is only the walking.
There is no one breathing,
There is no one walking.

Peace while breathing,
Peace while walking.
Peace is the breathing,
Peace is the walking.

WALKING WITH POEMS

You can walk using *gathas*, short practice poems. Combine your breath and your steps, and walk according to the rhythm of the poem. Arrange it so that the poems go rhythmically with your steps. Sometimes my in-breath is two steps and my out-breath is three steps. Sometimes my in-breath is three steps and my out-breath is four steps. Especially at the beginning, breathing out is always longer than breathing in. You can change the poem, adding or taking away words to match the rhythm of your steps. When you do jogging or running meditation, you can breathe in and make four steps, breathe out and make five steps. Dwell peacefully on the meaning of that poem in the present moment. Don't let your mind go far away. Don't try to be so poetic that you forget the practice. The main point of the practice is to cultivate more concentration.

In. Out.
Deep. Slow.
Calm. Ease.
Smile. Release.
Present moment.
Wonderful moment.

THE ISLAND OF SELF

The gatha I often take refuge in is, "Coming back to the island of myself." When life seems like a turbulent ocean, we have to remember we have an island of peace inside. Life has ups and downs, coming and going, gain and loss. Dwelling in the island of self, you are safe. When the Buddha was dying, he taught us not to take refuge in anything or anyone else, but to only take refuge in our own island. Breathing in, make two steps and say, "Taking refuge." Breathing out, make three steps and say, "In the island of self." Or change it to, "I go back. Taking refuge." You can always adjust whatever poem you've chosen to practice with.

Breathing in, I go back
to the island within myself.
There are beautiful trees
within the island.
There are clear streams of water.
There are birds,
sunshine and fresh air.
Breathing out, I feel safe.
I enjoy going back
to my island.

SLOW WALKING

When you are alone, you can practice slow walking meditation. Choose a distance of about three meters, or ten feet, and as you traverse that distance, take one step for each in-breath and one step for each out-breath. With the first step you can say silently, "I have arrived." With the next step, you can say silently, "I am home." If you aren't arriving one hundred percent in the here and now, stay there and don't make another step. Challenge yourself. Breathe in and out again until you feel you have arrived one hundred percent in the here and the now. Then smile a smile of victory. Then make a second step. This is to learn a new habit, the habit of living in the present moment.

FAMILY PRACTICE

Go out for a slow walk with your children
before going to sleep. Just ten minutes is
enough. If your children want to, you can
hold hands as you walk. Your child will
receive your concentration and stability,
and you will receive his or her innocence
and freshness. Young people might like
to practice this simple poem while they
walk. They can say to themselves, "Yes,
yes, yes," as they breathe in, and, "Thanks,
thanks, thanks," when they breathe out.
I know many children who like this poem
very much.

ARRIVING IN THE
PRESENT MOMENT

Some of us don't need to use words to help us concentrate, but in the beginning of the practice it can be very helpful to make use of words. They help us to be concentrated, to be in the here and the now. When you take one in-breath, make two steps, and say to yourself: "I have arrived. I have arrived." Take one out-breath and make three steps, and say to yourself: "I am home. I am home. I am home." This is not a statement; this is a practice. Arrive in the here and the now, and make a strong determination to stop and not to run anymore. You can say, "Arrived, arrived," as you breathe in, and, "Home, home, home," as you breathe out. After spending some time with "Arrived, home," you can change to, "Here, now," and then to, "Solid, free."

I have arrived.
I am home
in the here,
in the now.

I am solid.
I am free.
In the ultimate
I dwell.

THE BEAUTIFUL PATH

The mind can go in a thousand directions.
But on this beautiful path, I walk in peace.
With each step, a gentle wind blows.
With each step, a flower blooms.

The mind darts from one thing to another, like a monkey swinging from branch to branch without stopping to rest. Thoughts have millions of pathways, and we are forever pulled along by them into the world of forgetfulness. If we can transform our walking path into a field for meditation, our feet will take every step in full awareness, our breathing will be in harmony with our steps, and our minds will naturally be at ease. Every step we take will reinforce our peace and joy and cause a stream of calm energy to flow through us.

TAKING REFUGE IN THE EARTH

When we can come back to ourselves and
take refuge in our inner island, we become
a home for ourselves and we become
a refuge for others at the same time.
Walking with one hundred percent of your
body and mind can free you from anger,
fear, and despair. Each step can express
your love for the Earth. While walking,
you can say,

> With each step,
> I come home to the Earth.
> With each step,
> I return to my source.
> With each step,
> I take refuge in Mother Earth.

Or, as you walk, you can say,

I love the Earth.
I am in love with the Earth.

A LETTER TO THE EARTH

Dear Mother Earth,

Every time I step upon the Earth, I will train
myself to see that I am walking on you.
Every time I place my feet on the Earth, I
have a chance to be in touch with you and
with all your wonders. With every step
I can touch the fact that you aren't just
beneath me, dear Mother, but you are also
within me. Each mindful and gentle step
can nourish me, heal me, and bring me into
contact with myself and with you in the
present moment.

Walking in this spirit, I can experience awakening. I can awaken to the fact
that I am alive, and that life is a precious
miracle. I can awaken to the fact that I am

never alone and can never die. You are always there within me and around me at every step, nourishing me, embracing me, and carrying me far into the future. Dear Mother, I make the promise today to return your love and fulfill this wish by investing every step I take on you with love and tenderness. I am walking not merely on matter, but on spirit.

Also available from Rider.

How to Eat

Thich Nhat Hanh

THICH NHAT HANH

HOW TO
EAT

'THE FATHER OF MINDFULNESS'
IRISH TIMES

Thich Nhat Hanh invites us to eat mindfully, and shows how each mouthful can nourish us on many different levels. Eating joyfully feeds our sense of compassion and understanding, and helps us achieve a healthy weight.

ISBN 9781846045158

Order direct from www.penguin.co.uk

How to Love
Thich Nhat Hanh

Thich Nhat Hanh brings his signature clarity, compassion and humour to the thorny question of how to love. He shows us how to open our hearts to ourselves and embrace the world.

ISBN 9781846045172

Order direct from www.penguin.co.uk

How to Sit

Thich Nhat Hanh

THICH NHAT HANH

HOW TO
SIT

'THE FATHER OF MINDFULNESS'
IRISH TIMES

Thich Nhat Hanh considers the mechanics of posture and
breathing, and reveals how the simple act of sitting quietly, at
peace with ourselves and our surroundings, can be a powerful
way to strengthen our inner resources.

ISBN 9781846045141

Order direct from www.penguin.co.uk

How to Relax

Thich Nhat Hanh

In *How to Relax*, Thich Nhat Hanh explains how we can achieve deep relaxation, control stress and refresh our minds. He guides us towards healing and calm, at ease in our own company, so that we can all reap the benefits of relaxation no matter where we are.

ISBN 9781846045189

Order direct from www.penguin.co.uk